A CHRISTIAN VIEW OF ECONOMICS

MARION LORING

Exposition Press   *Smithtown, New York*

FIRST EDITION

© 1983 by Marion Loring

ISBN 0-682-49903-X

Printed in the United States of America

Contents

God the Creator

"In the Beginning God created . . . the earth."

Economics is concerned with the production of things man wants. Many economic texts start by saying that the main problem in economics is that resources are limited but man has unlimited wants. The obvious solution then is to be careful with our resources and curb our unlimited desires, as all the great religions and philosophies teach. Our present economic system does just the opposite. Our limited resources will last if we are careful and don't waste them. Some economists talk of nature being "niggardly." On the contrary, God our Father provides abundantly, but we waste.

Economics talks of three factors of production—land, labor, and capital. Land, in economics, is not just ordinary land but all that comes from the earth. In fact it includes water, sun, minerals, and wild animals—all things that God created.

LAND

Consider the Old Testament teaching on land: "The earth is the Lord's." He gives it to people on certain conditions, not outright:

1.   Land belongs to God who gives it. "I will give to you and your descendants this land in which you are now a foreigner"

(Gen. 17:8). "Your land must not be sold on a permanent basis, because you do not own it; it belongs to God, and you are like foreigners who are allowed to make use of it" (Lev. 25:23).

2. Land is given to the tribe and family rather than the individual. "Moses had given a part of the land to the families of the tribe of Reuben as their possession" (Josh. 13:15). If a man had to sell land he was supposed to sell it to a relative. "And in all the country you possess, you shall grant a redemption of the land. If your brother becomes poor, and sells part of his property, then his next of kin shall come and redeem what his brother has sold" (Lev. 25:23-25). "Boaz said, 'Very well, if you buy the field from Naomi, then you are also buying Ruth, the Moabite widow, so that the field will stay in the dead man's family' " (Ruth 4:5). Even a king could not take it legally: " 'I inherited this vineyard from my ancestors,' Naboth replied to King Ahab. 'The Lord forbid that I should let you have it!' " (1 Kings 21:3).

3. Land must be cared for, its fertility preserved. "Six years you shall sow your field, and six years you shall prune your vineyard, and gather in its fruits; but in the seventh year there shall be a sabbath of solemn rest for the land, a sabbath to the Lord; you shall not sow your field or prune your vineyard" (Lev. 26:3-4). There was a punishment for not obeying this. "But if you will not hearken to me, and will not do all these commandments, . . . I will scatter you among the nations. Then the land shall enjoy its sabbaths as long as it lies desolate, while you are in your enemies' land" (Lev. 26:33-34). Does this principle perhaps apply to our practice of using good agricultural land for roads and buildings?

Our concept of land should not be that it is a commodity to be bought and sold, but that God has made it for our use. We own only what we produce from it and hold it in trust for others as stewards. "Unused fields could yield plenty of food for the poor, but unjust men keep them from being farmed" (Prov. 13:23).

4. Land should be evenly distributed. It was not considered good for too much land to be in the possession of big landowners. Isaiah said, "Therefore in the Year of Jubilee any land that had been bought should be returned to the original family" (Isa. 5:8).

"In this way you shall set the fiftieth year apart and proclaim freedom to all the inhabitants of the land. During this year all property that has been sold shall be restored to the original owner or his descendants" (Lev. 25:10). This recognized the basic right of everyone to enough land to grow the food they needed. This law of Jubilee is especially noteworthy: all debts were to be forgiven and land that had been sold returned to the original family. We talk about preserving the family farm, but we're not doing it. And we can't just blame agribusiness. As Isaiah said, "Woe to those who join house to house, who add field to field, until there is no more room, and you are made to dwell alone in the midst of the land" (Isa. 5:8). The intent of the Homestead Act was for everyone to have the opportunity to own enough land to make an independent living. This intent was spoiled by an economic system that demands mass production, and by permitting the sale of land to anyone, foreigner or speculator.

OWNERSHIP

Since we have not made the land or its natural resources, the question of ownership is pertinent. "The Earth is the Lord's." Have we the right to put a fence around a part and say, "This is mine"? The hunter-gatherers did not need to; it is only when men have sown seeds that they've needed to, in order to protect the seeds and have the right to the produce. Ownership is not to be of the land itself but of the fruit of the work done on the land. The old concept of public, not private, ownership still often applies to water, forests, wild animals, and minerals.

Man is not supposed to dominate the land then, only cultivate it. Adam was put into the Garden of Eden to till it. It is interesting to notice the word *cult* in *cultivate*. A cult is a system of worship, and in Hebrew the word for *worship* is the same as the word 'to till' (the soil). Another meaning of the word *cultivate* is 'to give time, thought, and effort' (*Dictionary of Canadian English*). The word *Adam* means 'human' and is the masculine form of Adamah, which means 'earth'. All this indicates that we should take a very humble attitude towards the earth, and should give thought to it.

MAN AND NATURE

People often say that the concept of man as one with nature is found only in other religions and not in Judeo-Christian teaching, but this is not so. That concept is tied in with the belief in the One Creator who made all things, plants, animals, and man. Man was not made on a separate day but on the same day as the animals.

Consider these passages and the picture they draw of nature—animate and inanimate—joining with man in praising God. "The wolf shall dwell with the lamb, and the leopard shall lie down with the kid, and the calf and the lion and the fatling together, and a little child shall lead them. The cow and the bear shall feed; their young shall lie down together, and the lion shall eat straw like the ox" (Isa. 11:6,7). "For you shall go out in joy, and be led forth in peace; the mountains and the hills before you shall break forth into singing, and all the trees of the field shall clap their hands" (Isa. 55:12). "When the morning stars sang together, and all the sons of God shouted for joy . . . to bring rain on a land where no man is, on the desert in which there is no man" (Job 38:7, 26). "Let the heavens be glad and let the earth rejoice; let the sea roar, and all that fills it; let the field exalt, and everything in it! Then shall all of the trees of the woods sing for joy" (Ps. 96:11-12). "Thou makest springs gush forth in the valleys; they flow between the hills, they give drink to every beast of the field; the wild asses quench their thirst" (Ps. 104:10-11). "I know all the birds of the air, and all that moves in the field is mine" (Ps. 50:11). "The heavens are telling the glory of God; and the firmament proclaims his handiwork. Day to day pours forth speech, and night to night declares knowledge. There is no speech, nor are there words; their voice is not heard; yet their voice goes out through all the earth, and their words to the end of the world. In them he has set a tent for the sun, which comes forth like a bridegroom leaving his chamber, and like a strong man runs its course with joy. Its rising is from the end of them; and there is nothing hid from its heat" (Ps. 19:1-6).

DOMINION

Some Christians have assumed that we are entitled to destroy nature. They quote, "Then God said, 'Let us make man in our image, after our likeness; and let them have dominion over the fish of the sea, and over the birds of the air, and over the cattle, and over all the earth . . ." (Gen. 1:26).

I have been a Christian for 70 years and I have attended church regularly, but it is only just recently that I have heard this text quoted as giving man the right to exploit the earth, and I have never heard it interpreted thus by a minister.

What does this word *dominion* mean? It comes from the Latin word *dominus* meaning 'lord', so it means lordship, having authority over a particular domain. When we call God "The Lord" we mean that He has supreme authority over all. Man is given the same sort of relationship to animals that God has to us. We see this concept vividly in the Twenty-third Psalm. "The Lord is my shepherd" means He is to me as a man is to his sheep. "He feeds me in a green pasture and leads me forth beside the still waters." How does God exercise His dominion? By caring for, feeding, and protecting the sheep. "I will fear no evil for thou art with me." The sheep don't fear when the shepherd is there.

ANIMALS

H. V. Morton[1] has written a vivid description of a shepherd in Bible lands, which he visited in the thirties.

> A most remarkable thing is the sympathy that exists between him and his flock. He never drives them as our own shepherds drive their sheep. He always walks at their head, leading them along the roads and over the hills to new pasture: and, as he goes, he sometimes talks to them in a loud sing-song voice, using a weird language unlike anything I have ever heard in my life.
>
> The man, accompanied by this animal, walked on and

disappeared around a ledge of rock. Very soon a panic spread among the herd. They forgot to eat. They looked up for the shepherd. He was not to be seen. They became conscious that the leader with the bell at his neck was no longer with them. From the distance came the strange laughing call of the shepherd, and at the sound of it the entire herd stampeded into the hollow and leapt up the hill after him.

Isaiah gives a picture of a similar type. "Behold, the Lord God comes with might. . . . He will feed His flock like a shepherd, He will gather the lambs in His arms, He will carry them in His bosom, and gently lead those that are with young" (Isa. 40:10-11).

Jesus said, "I am the good shepherd; I know my own and my own know me, as the Father knows me and I know the Father; and I lay down my life for the sheep" (John 10:14-15).

This is God's idea of lordship. Jesus refused to be the sort of king that the people wanted, to lead them against the Romans; He was King of Love, crowned on the cross. He said to His disciples, "You call me Lord and Master and you say right for so I am. If I then your Lord and Master have washed your feet, you ought also to wash one another's feet."

Sheep are mentioned frequently in the Bible, but never do men speak of them as just production units as we do now. The possession of animals is a sign of wealth. "Now Abram was very rich in cattle, in silver, and in gold" (Gen. 13:2). But there are regulations against exploitation: "You shall not muzzle the ox that treads out the grain" and "You shall not boil a kid in its mother's milk." (Deut. 22:6). "If you chance to come upon a bird's nest, in any tree or on the ground, with young ones or eggs and the mother sitting upon the young or upon the eggs, you shall not take the mother with the young" (Deut. 22:6). So it is rule, not ownership, for God says, "For every beast of the forest is mine, the cattle on a thousand hills" (Ps. 50:10). Jesus said, "Look at the birds of the air: they neither sow nor reap nor gather into barns and yet your heavenly Father feeds them. Are you not of more value than they? Are not two sparrows sold for a penny? And not one of them will fall to the ground without your Father" (Matt. 6:26, 10:29). This implies individual care for each one.

Christians should be concerned with animal conservation, remembering that the first example of that is in the story of Noah's Ark. They should be concerned with being kind to animals and preserving a good relationship with them. In the past, people used to give their cows names. In mass production systems they are just numbers, and this indicates that there is no longer a personal relationship. This passage from Genesis (2:18-19) is illuminating: "Then the Lord God said, 'It is not good that the man should be alone; I will make him a helper fit for him.' So out of the ground the Lord God formed every beast of the field and every bird of the air, and brought them to the man to see what he would call them; and whatever the man called every living creature, that was its name."

Now Jesus' interpretation of the Old Testament was of fulfilling, that is, completing, filling full, obeying the spirit of the law, not just the letter. So Christians should fill these passages full. As G. K. Chesterton[2] pointed out, Christianity went through a time when the ideas of flowers and birds were played down, because they were associated with the worship of sun and moon and the use of flowers in worship; not in the simple nature worship of its beginning, but first in sophisticated orgies of an effete Roman empire under which Christians had been persecuted, and then, after the fall of Rome, in the Germanic religions of the barbarians who invaded Western Europe, killing and conquering.

After these dark ages, the sun shone again, and simple Christians like Francis of Assisi were able to worship God in nature again. Mrs. Oliphant,[3] in her biography of this saint, wrote: "Not only was every man his brother, but every animal—the sheep in the fields, the birds in the branches, the brother-ass on which he rode, the sister-bees who took refuge in his kind protection. He turned, sick at heart, from the perpetual strife and contention of his time, from fighting cities, rapacious nobles, a whole world of blood and oppression, and, with an unspeakable relief, heard the gentle birds singing in the woods, the harmless creatures rustling among the trees. . . . They were God's harmless, voiceless folk, who knew His name, and sang His praises. . . . This thought runs through the whole theory of existence as recognized by Francis and men of like mind. They could not doubt that where God had put life, He had also put the consciousness of Himself."

In the Renaissance, the sense of freedom and naturalness led to a flowering of poetry about nature in religion, for example, Dunbar's "On the Nativity of Christ"[4]:

> *Celestial fowls in the air,*
> *Sing with your notes upon high,*

and Vaughan's "The Bird"[5]:

> *So hills and valleys into singing break;*
> *And though poor stones have neither speech nor tongue,*
> *While active winds and streams both run and speak,*
> *Yet stones are deep in admiration.*
> *Thus praise and prayer here beneath the sun*
> *Make lesser mornings, when the great are done.*

IMPERIALISM

Ever since the Renaissance the educated men of Europe have been taught the classics, that is, the literature of pre-Christian Greece and Rome. They acquired from it some increased intellectual freedom and appreciation of nature, but they have been taught to look on the Roman Empire as the height of civilization. The Romans believed that dominion gave them the right to exploit. They forced conquered countries to pay tribute, and they exploited their human resources by dragging away thousands of people as slaves. They turned much of Northern Africa into desert by cutting down trees and cultivating grain.

We have not considered the effect of this education in Roman literature—including the writings of Caesar the conqueror, Livy the historian, and Cicero the lawyer—on Western economic thought. I believe that the imperialism of some European countries has been largely due to this. The influence of Rome was also seen on the plantations of the southern states, run on slave labor as were the Roman villa plantations. In the Roman Empire, private possession of land was an accepted idea, which it was not in medieval days. Rome had a capitalist system.

But this admiration for Imperial Rome and the imitation of its ruthless type of domination was in conflict with many Christian principles. This conflict still exists, though we would call it more the conflict between the materialism, greed and self-interest of capitalism and the more gentle, altruistic, spiritual ideals of Christianity. The British rule over its colonies and the poor in Britain was not based only on trade and domination, but was tempered by other ideas. The campaign for the abolition of slavery under William Wilberforce, the humanitarian reforms pushed by Shaftesbury, Owen, Elizabeth Fry, and the medical and educational work of Florence Nightingale, Livingstone, Matthew Arnold, Mary Slessor and other missionaries—all were the triumph of the Christian ideals. There was also the Anglo-Saxon ideal, accentuated by Greek studies, for freedom and democracy, which came through in the vernacular literature and popular education. Some of the elite, who wanted to maintain domination of the colonies, objected to the teaching of English by missionaries on the ground that the natives would thus learn to want freedom! But it remained an ideal, and some of the young district officers sent out by the British Colonial Office had that ideal and really tried to help the native people.

THE FATHER

This conflict between the capitalist/imperialist concept of dominion and the Christian/democratic one is crucial. Capitalism is based on self-interest, profit maximization, competition, and survival of the fittest, and imperialism assumes that the strong have a right to exploit the weak. But the Christian ideal is that dominion should be that of a father who cares for his children but encourages them to be themselves and to have as much freedom as they can handle satisfactorily. This ideal of freedom is seen in the principle that one is not born a Christian, but is asked to accept the faith voluntarily and individually.

Soldiers have said that there are two kinds of officers, the "come-ons," and the "go-ons." Christ was a come-on, as He went alone to the Cross, then said "Come, follow me." Eric Fromm talks of the two types of authority, first the authority of parent over child, and teacher over pupil, and second that of master over slave and boss over employee. The characteristics of the first are that it is intended to be for the good of the subordinate, the child, and that it is not permanent, for the child will naturally grow out of it. The characteristics of the second are that it is for the benefit of the employer and that employees usually stay in the employee position. Christian dominion is intended to be of the first kind, the fatherly kind.

God the Father provides food for the sparrows, beautiful clothes for the flowers, enough natural resources to satisfy all our needs. He has given us the intelligence to use these natural resources efficiently. He has also given us free will, but many of us are using that to break His laws, waste and pollute the resources, and fight greedily for more than we need. If we obey His Commandments, to love Him and each other, and not to lay up treasure on earth, we will be able to enjoy nature's abundance. Kipling,[6] in his wonderful hymn, "Recessional," has the right words for this:

> Beneath Whose Aweful Hand we hold
> Dominion over palm and pine.
> Lord God of Hosts, be with us yet
> Lest we forget. Lest we forget.

It is a reminder to imperial powers that the powerful Hand that gives authority will be the One to punish if that authority is abused . . .

> If, drunk with sight of power, we loose
> Wild tongues that have not Thee in awe,
> Lord God of Hosts, be with us yet,
> Lest we forget, lest we forget.

2

God the Carpenter

LABOR

"Come unto me, all you who labor and are heavy laden and I will give you rest!" (Matt. 11:28).

Both capitalism and communism assume that the majority of people own only one of the means of production, namely their own labor, which they must "sell" to an employer in return for a wage that is all they have to live on. So employment becomes a major issue. But in the past the majority had land and simple capital and could work to produce for themselves instead of for an employer.

The Third Commandment tells us *not* to do any work on the seventh day, but to rest, and Jesus said, "The Sabbath was made for man and not man for the Sabbath." So we see that God wants us to work, but not too hard.

THE WORK ETHIC

The so-called Protestant work ethic teaches that the more work you do, the better you are, regardless of whether that work is really necessary or good for society.

Max Weber[1] compares the traditional attitude whereby a man

11

was concerned with "how the customary wage may be earned with a maximum of comfort and a minimum of exertion" with the capitalist one whereby "labour must, on the contrary, be performed as if it were an absolute end in itself, a calling." He describes the more leisurely way of doing business as the idyllic state that "collapsed under the pressure of a bitter competitive struggle."

I have sometimes been reproved by economists for using the word *ought*. Yet it is a curious fact that both capitalism and communism claim to be scientific and pragmatic, having no affair with ethics, and yet they both teach that the workers *ought* to do their best, that work is a *good* thing, that everyone *ought* to be employed.

These principles are also found in the Bible. "Whatever your task, work heartily, as serving the Lord, not man" (Col. 3:23). "We kept working day and night so as not to be an expense to any of you. We did this, not because we do not have the right to demand our support; we did it to be an example for you to follow. While we were with you, we used to tell you, 'Whoever refuses to work is not allowed to eat' " (2 Thess. 3:6). Moreover, the duty of supporting a family is taught. "But if anyone does not take care of his relatives, especially the members of his own family, he has denied the faith and is worse than an unbeliever" (1 Tim. 5:8). But the reasons given here are firstly to please God by doing to His glory whatever has to be done, and secondly so as not to be a burden on other people. Work for its own sake, or in order to get on top, is not taught. If your work is to be pleasing to God it should obviously be a good sort of work, but the capitalist principle is generally that any kind of work is good and the more money it earns the better it is, since money is the measure of value.

The Protestant work ethic seems to have been based on the idea put forward by both Calvin and Wesley, that people should be made to work in order to keep them out of mischief. This is a negative idea. In the story of Adam, he is first put in the Garden to cultivate it, but it is only when he is sent away from Eden that he has to earn bread by the sweat of his brow. This implies that the work in the Garden was easy, and Adam and Eve had time to walk in the Garden and talk to God. When we have less work, we should have more time for prayer. But the work ethic was also a reaction to the idea that just praying and meditating and depending on others to provide one's food was better, and that rich people who didn't work were superior. This is not Christian teaching.

CHRIST'S EXAMPLE

Jesus himself set an example in labor. It appears that He worked as a simple village carpenter till He was about thirty. After that His work was preaching and healing, but He was not a "professional" preacher or doctor with the usual education for it. So in His life, He hallowed manual work and simple service to people. We tend, as many other societies do also, to think manual work inferior, and intellectual work better. Followers of the Carpenter of Nazareth cannot rightly believe that. If we despise the laborer, we are despising Jesus.

When Jesus was preaching and healing, He certainly did work very hard and so did His followers, but that was doing what needed to be done urgently. Jesus healed even on the Sabbath not for pay, nor because He had to do busywork but because people needed to be healed. Christians need to work hard at evangelizing and setting an example to others of a good type of work of benefit to society, but they should not do busywork.

I would like to talk particularly about personal service. The world usually regards this as inferior work, but a Christian should not. Jesus said, "The Son of Man came not to be ministered unto, but to minister." And to minister means to serve. He washed His disciples' feet. He said, "Whoever would be greatest among you, let him be your servant."

I used to serve as a waitress in resort hotels during the summer holidays, and I found pleasure in the thought that by doing my work cheerfully and efficiently I could help to make people's holidays better. Why should the impersonal work of a government typist be considered superior to the personal work of a cleaning woman who comes to your house and helps you? The latter is classified as unskilled, but she isn't—she learned skills at home from her mother.

Christians should improve their attitude to personal service. It would be good if some of us were to take up this sort of work deliberately as a means of serving humanity. We must not despise the jobs of garbage collectors, waitresses, and so forth. But until we have changed our attitude we may do harm if we push unemployed people into these jobs. Encouraging repair work by giving training and ideas may be more important.

The Christian work ethic should be that we should work wholeheartedly at the things that need doing, that are of service to others, but not rush around doing unnecessary things. The time saved by having machines do work for us can be devoted to spiritual matters, as Mary did, rather than like Martha, who was "distracted with much serving." Many Christians today, brought up under our materialistic work ethic, think that Martha was in the right and Mary was in the wrong; that is to contradict Jesus. God will provide the material necessities of life without excessive toil. The greatest luxury is to have spiritual "treasure in heaven."

THE EMPLOYEES

Those who have their own land or capital can labor for the livelihood of their families. But the landless man, who has to work for a wage, has always been subject to exploitation unless he has a high degree of skill. In the past, many of them were slaves; even though not officially so, pauper children employed by mill owners in England were really slaves. Dictators of today find other means of forcing people to work for starvation wages. The Bible has many examples of this. "Hear this, you who trample upon the needy, and bring the poor of the land to an end, saying, 'When will the new moon be over, that we may sell grain? And the sabbath, that we may offer wheat for sale, that we may make the ephah small and the shekel great, and deal deceitfully with false balances, that we may buy the poor for silver and the needy for a pair of sandals, and sell the refuse of the wheat?' " (Amos 8:4-6). "Now there arose a great outcry of the people and of their wives against their Jewish brethren. For there were those who said, 'With our sons and our daughters, we are many; let us get grain, that we may eat and keep alive.' There were also those that said, 'We are mortgaging our fields, our vineyards and our houses to get grain because of the famine.' And there were those who said, 'We have borrowed money for the king's tax upon our fields and our vineyards. Now our flesh is as the flesh of our brethren, our children are as their children; yet we are forcing our sons and daughters to be slaves, and some of our daughters have already been enslaved; but it is not in our power to help it, for other men have our fields and our vineyards.' I was very angry when I heard their outcry and these words. I took counsel with myself, and I brought charges against the nobles and the officials. I said to them, 'You are exacting interest, each from his brother.' And I held a great assembly against them" (Neh. 5:1-7). "The Lord enters into judgement with the elders and princes of His people: 'It is you who have devoured the vineyard, the spoil of the poor is in your houses. What do you mean by crushing my people, by grinding the face of the poor?' says the Lord God of Hosts" (Isa. 3:14-15).

We see here that poverty and slavery were caused chiefly by powerful men taking land from the weak. It was then the landless that were exploited. In Britain the nobility expropriated the common land under the Enclosures Act and thereby forced the poor to go to the towns to seek work. So now there are millions of people with nothing but their labor, depending on someone paying them for it so that they can buy the food they can no longer produce for themselves.

Goods are produced by labor from natural resources. If a man cannot get access to these resources, he cannot produce, except under the power of those who own them. So everyone ought to have the right to the tools and materials of production. But, especially for those who live in cities, access to the means of exchanging their goods for food is another essential. So a really free type of market is important.

TRADE UNIONS

It is this utter dependence of the poor that impelled them to band together in unions to demand better conditions. It may perhaps be argued that the strike, which is the withholding of labor from those who need it, is similar to withholding the land, but the land is God's, labor is individual. Moreover, unions generally agree that really vital work should not be stopped. The worst feature of strikes today is that the successful ones are mostly by big unions whose members get average pay, while the really poor workers' strikes don't often succeed. The rich unions should help the poorer ones and not insist on their "historic differential." It is the adversary attitude that is so wrong. It came about because so many employers did exploit shamefully, and so bred suspicion and hatred that cannot easily be overcome. Christians should try to engender better attitudes, but it must begin with a real change of heart among employers.

The most notable biblical example of withdrawal of labor occurs in the great story of the Exodus from Egypt, where God tells the people to leave. This story is an inspiration to thousands of oppressed people today.

Unity is taught in the Bible through the concept of brotherhood, which is of course a natural outcome of the concept of a heavenly Father. So there is nothing wrong with singing "Solidarity Forever." It would be good if employers could join in.

COMMUNISM

However, the Bible does teach that we should trust God rather than man. He tells the rich to share with the poor: He does not tell the poor to take from the rich as communism does. In Latin America, we are seeing that the Church's championship of the poor, landless people is having some effect. But sometimes priests are falsely labelled "communists," when they help the poor. This is foolish, as it plays into the hands of the communists by showing them to be the helpers of the poor. If the rich landowners there do not heed the Church's teaching, communists may become like Assyrians of old, a heathen people whom God used to punish the rulers of Israel, as Isaiah prophesied (Isa. 10:1-6): "Woe to those who decree iniquitous decrees, and the writers who keep writing oppression, to turn aside the needy from justice and to rob the poor of my people of their right, that widows may be their spoil, and that they may make the fatherless their prey! What will you do on the day of punishment, in the storm which will come from afar? To whom will you flee for help, and where will you leave your wealth? Nothing remains but to crouch among the prisoners or fall among the slain. For all this his anger is not turned away and his hand is stretched out still. Ah, Assyria, the rod of my anger, the staff of my fury! Against a godless nation I send him, and against the people of my wrath I command him, to take spoil and seize plunder, and to tread them down like the mire of the streets." This prophecy was fulfilled as we read in 2 Chronicles, 33:10-11: "The Lord spoke to Manasseh and to His people but they gave no heed. Therefore the Lord brought upon them the commanders of the army of the king of Assyria, who took Manasseh with hooks and bound him with fetters of bronze and brought him to Babylon." God did not approve of Assyria, but used it; He does not approve of communism, but may use it.

But communism also orders that most people own only their own labor, not land or capital, and must be employed by the state. So it is contrary to the biblical concept of man's labor being used on the land given him by God to provide for his family.

CITY FOLK

The majority of people now living in cities cannot go back to the land. What has Christianity to say about labor in cities?

There is a curious ambivalence in the Bible's attitude to cities. On the one hand they seem to be regarded as the epitome of evil: yet on the other it is Jerusalem that is the center of worship and of the Jews' love for their country. In Revelation, Heaven is described as the New Jerusalem. And indeed in cities today we find the most appalling conditions of poverty and crime side by side with the beauties of civilization. The pyramids were built by slave labor. Are all artistic and engineering feats of mankind possible only by exploitation? Not with modern technology, certainly.

In cities there are the greatest possibilities for evil and the severest temptations. But there are also the greatest possibilities for good, the highest hopes. Which will triumph, good or evil? This depends on whether the rich share with the poor, so that the poor, unskilled laborer can have an equal chance for happiness. And remember that a skilled employee, who gets high pay, is also one of the rich. Certainly here in North America, there is no need for poverty; we have abundance, we can train our unskilled workers, and pay well for the unskilled work that really needs to be done. It is well known that the children of the poor seldom become rich. This shows that they don't get an equal opportunity. All this is a matter of justice, and that is certainly a biblical concept.

Jesus, the Carpenter, was not a landowner, but a craftsman, serving the village people and accepting pay from them (probably sometimes in kind). He therefore hallowed this type of labor. Who deserves more pay, Pontius Pilate the governor, or Jesus the Carpenter? Which one do we think superior? Whom do we really worship?

3

God the Inspirer

CAPITAL

There are three kinds of capital: physical, intellectual, and financial.

1. Physical—Capital goods are the things we make, not for consumption, but to enable us to produce more. So when a Stone Age hunter took time to make a better arrowhead, he was creating capital so he would then be able to kill more animals. When a peasant saved some grain that could have been used for bread, that was capital: it was thrown into the ground as seed so more grain would grow the following year. That is the meaning of the text, "He who sows in tears (because he was depriving himself of bread) will reap in joy." We still use the expression "seed capital" for the money used to start up a business and that does not bring in a return till later. So capital is still basically tools and seed. It includes also the tools of transportation, cars, ships, roads, and so forth. It also includes factories and the great machines in them.

To whom do these things belong originally? Generally, we would say to the person who makes them. All physical capital is made by humans from natural resources, that is, by labor from land. The labor of those who make the machines must be rewarded.

19

2. Intellectual—Something more than just labor is needed: a horse can do work, but to make tools requires man's thought, imagination, and ingenuity. The first arrow maker used his creative capacities, he taught his skill to others.

Who invented the first wheel? We don't know, but this invention has been passed on from generation to generation with numerous extra ideas and adaptations, and we've inherited all these ideas. Much of our capital, therefore, may be said to belong to all humanity. Even our physical capital is partly mental. Knowledge is capital, for we don't improve production just by having tools but by knowing how to use them. By reading and writing, this knowledge is passed on; mathematics and geography help us to improve production and transportation. So education is also capital, and the things we learn have come to us from the Egyptians, the Greeks, the Arabs, the Romans, and many others.

Why does the peasant refrain from eating the grain and throw it back in the soil? Because he has been taught by his parents that he will then have more next year. It is the result of knowledge about investment—that one grain can become twenty grains. This capital is inherited; it depends on language, creativity, organization, and so forth.

C. H. Douglas[1] wrote this about cultural heritage: "And since it is a cultural legacy, it seems difficult to deny that the general community, as a whole, and not by any qualification of land, labour, or capital, are the proper legatees." This is particularly true when inventions result from an educational system that has been paid for by society.

3. Financial—We tend to equate capital with money, but this is incorrect. It is not just money, for money is not real wealth, it is bits of paper, or figures in a bank ledger representing real wealth. Wealth consists of the things we buy with money and the real things we have done to earn it. Money depends on symbolism, on our capacity to write figures and add and subtract.

Financial capital is similar to the seed of the peasant, who invests the saved grain. The man who saves money and invests it expects to get an increase. But this won't happen if the money is kept idle in a bank. For a real increase it must be used to produce real goods or services, that is, changed back into physical or mental capital.

Money is essentially social, for it demands a total society in which it is accepted as a symbol for a certain value. It depends on trade, which is a social activity. Our banking system depends on credit, which means trust, for banks must trust borrowers to repay the loan. It depends on saving—looking to the future. So it is basically mental, also.

INSPIRATION

"See, the Lord has called by name Bez'ales, the son of Uri, son of Hur, of the tribe of Judah; and he has filled him with the Spirit of God, with ability, with intelligence, with knowledge, and with all craftsmanship, to devise artistic designs, to work in gold and silver and bronze, in cutting stones for setting, and in carving wood, for work in every skilled craft. And he has inspired him to teach" (Exod. 35:30-34). Many inventions, as well as literature and art, have been inspired by "the spirit of wisdom and understanding, the spirit of counsel and might, the spirit of knowledge and the fear of the Lord" (Isa. 11:2). This is the best kind of capital.

When men in Babel tried by their own engineering, without fear of the Lord, to build "a tower with its top in heaven" (Gen. 11:4), they failed and could no longer understand each other. But in the account of the coming of the Spirit at Pentecost, we are told of the different languages the people spoke, though they were all able to understand Peter. The cultural heritage is passed on through learning and understanding. The description of the coming of the Holy Spirit at Pentecost shows that the Holy Spirit is God within man, for the "cloven tongues of fire" show the One Spirit dividing up and coming in each person. The Church is essentially the society that is one in the Spirit. God the Father is God above us making the laws of nature; God the Son is God walking on the earth before and beside us setting us an example; God the Spirit is God inside us making us an inspired society.

EASING THE BURDEN

Of he who has the seven spirits it says: ". . . but with righteousness he shall judge the poor, and decide with equity for the meek of the earth" (Isa. 11:4). Revelation talks of the seven golden lampstands, which are the seven churches, and of the seven lamps of fire, which are the seven spirits of God. So the churches that have the seven spirits should use their capital to give justice and equity to the poor and meek of the earth, to ease their burden of work and increase production to take away their poverty. Labor is individual, but much of capital is inherited and belongs to all humanity.

An article in *New Internationalist*[2] says:

> For millions of women in Africa, Asia and Latin America the working day begins commonly at 4:30 or 5:00 A.M. and ends sixteen hours later, as they struggle to meet the most basic needs of their families—for food, water, firewood, clothes, health care and a home. The reason for this "hundred-hour week" is that most women do two jobs in the home and in agriculture. . . . Most of the agricultural training and technology has been geared to men's work.

Our capital could ease that burden. Instead, most capital is put into manufacturing that takes work away from craftsmen, leaving them with no work at all or with dull, repetitive work, while others still work too hard. As long as the prime objective of capital is to earn maximum profits for capitalists, this will continue. Capital should be used to ease the burden of hard work and to provide more of the things people need. Knowledge, wisdom, counsel, and might enable us to do this, but we must also have the fear of the terrible consequences of breaking God's commandments.

INTEREST

This raises the question of interest on capital. In the Old
Testament, Jews were forbidden to charge interest to fellow Jews.
Jesus said, "Lend, ask nothing in return" (Luke 6:35). The
medieval Church therefore prohibited interest absolutely. It is
sometimes said that the Protestants opened the gates to it, but
even the Papacy had practiced it although it was condemned. As
Tawney describes in *Religion and the Rise of Capitalism*[3]: "Luther
was vehement against it. He said, 'The greatest misfortune of the
German nation is easily the traffic in interest. . . . The devil invented it, and the Pope, by giving his sanction to it, has done
untold evil throughout the world.' "

Calvin, according to Tawney,[4] "taught that interest is lawful,
provided that it does not exceed an official maximum, that, even
when a maximum is fixed, loans must be made gratis to the poor,
that the borrower must reap as much advantage as the lender, that
excessive security must not be exacted, that what is venial as an
occasional expedient is reprehensible when carried on as a regular
occupation; that no man may snatch economic gain for himself
to the injury of his neighbor." Tawney adds that "a condonation
of usury protected by such embarrassing entanglements can have
offered but tepid consolation to the devout money-lender!"

We should think carefully about this. Consider also the difference between the man who invests his own savings in a business
that he himself runs, and the man who invests money and sits
back and takes in the profit made by the labor of others. Should
they not share the profit?

FINANCE

Capital, which used to be the tool of a man's trade, and the
owner-manager's own investment, has come too much in the hands
of the rich financiers. Indeed, all these takeover bids by giant firms
show that real productive business is being subordinated to the
financiers' lust for power. Dr. Carter, Secretary-General of the

Royal Economic Society, wrote[5] that "wealth in money and stocks and shares is not tied closely to the flow or stock of real goods. . . . The interests of the holders of paper wealth do not necessarily lie in the same direction as the interests of the nation as a producer of real things." However, with the increase in miniaturized technology and the stress on appropriate, or intermediate, technology, there is hope that we can return before long to production by and for humans to whom our cultural heritage belongs. Small businesses run by people who are interested in producing goods are better, and with electricity in the home and so many good, small, electric tools, do-it-yourself production is already beginning to come back, and we should encourage these trends.

WISDOM

Church members in the industrialized world have human capital: spirit and knowledge; and physical capital in the form of goods and money. Some of this was acquired by taking land from others (for example, enclosures in England and the conquest of Indians in America) or exploiting colonies. Some has come from our inherited knowledge. Some through our own work. The Church, in its development projects, tries to pass this on, but we need the spirit of wisdom and understanding to do it well.

Think again of "the spirit of wisdom and understanding, the spirit of counsel and might, the spirit of knowledge and the fear of the Lord." The essence of wisdom is, I think, an intuitive understanding of life, based on inspiration and experience, and especially an understanding of people. Science gives us knowledge of atomic energy, but it needs wisdom to know how to use it for the good of humanity. It needs also the fear of the Lord. Fear is a warning of danger, danger of going contrary to the will of God, who knows what is best for us. We need to fear the danger of using scientific discoveries without knowing their long-term effects. We need to take counsel together before we use our might. Counsel implies talking together, cooperating. We should share our technology and work together as children of One Father, instead of competing, and we should try to bring forth the fruits of the Spirit: "love, joy, peace, patience, kindness, goodness, faithfulness, gentleness, self-control" (Gal. 5:22). If we "walk by the Spirit, and do not gratify the desires of the flesh," we shall not seek so many material things, but realize that the best luxuries are the spiritual "treasures in Heaven." We shall not then have the unlimited wants that cause economic problems, and our capital can be a blessing to the rich and the poor by easing their burdens and giving them time to enjoy God.

4

Shalom or Competition?

The Bible sets before us Life, Light, and Goodness, contrasted with Death, Darkness, and Evil, and bids us to choose. In more scientific language, we might speak of harmony or chaos, creation or destruction, orderliness or entropy. One fundamental difference between life and nonlife is that life tends to orderliness, which is harmony of different parts working together. Plants and animals have a blueprint in their genes and develop according to plan; plan implies purpose that comes from personal will. But all nonliving things are subject to the law of entropy, the second law of thermodynamics. They tend inexorably to chaos, a mix-up, a complete lack of order as in smoke and dust. Energy ceases to cause movement or work when heat and cold are mixed to be just lukewarm. For it is the difference in temperature that causes movement, as we see when we open the door on a cold day and the hot air rushes out while the cold comes in. Energy for work, once used up, becomes completely useless and can never be used again. It cannot be recycled. By burning oil, instead of using it for fertilizer, we hasten the process towards entropic chaos, which is the final death of the earth. Life and nonlife move in opposite directions.

But the sun pours energy upon us continually, and as long as the sun lasts we shall not lack. The sun helps the fruit to grow; we eat, and have its energy for work. If we were to work only to produce more food to enable us to work more, we would be tending to entropy also, for death of body comes in the end to all living things. But we use our energy also to enjoy life, to dance and sing, to talk and exchange ideas, to pray and praise. These nonmaterial results of work are the everlasting ones. Spiritual energy is not subject to entropy. The Spirit of God can always move on the face of the waters, and dispel the chaos and darkness there as described in Genesis 1:1. The heat and smoke that ascend from the fire can no more be used as energy to produce work, but the biblical image of the smoke of sacrifice ascending to God reminds us that our life is not just work. The duty of humans, as the old Presbyterian catechism told us, is to worship God and enjoy Him forever.

But nature shows also movement in cycles, such as the rain, carbon dioxide, and nitrogen cycles. Plants and animals live in interdependence as plants breathe in carbon dioxide and give out oxygen; animals breathe in oxygen, giving back carbon dioxide to the plants. The rain cycle depends only on gravity and the sun: the nitrogen and the carbon dioxide cycles depend on the work of the plants, which are the producers of food, and on the co-operation of plants and animals.

Dr. P. Craigie,[1] speaking on ancient wisdom at the Banff Conference on Man and His Environment, described one tenet of ancient wisdom common to nearly all religions:

> In some way . . . human morality is inextricably mixed with cosmology, or to put that differently, one cannot think of morality or develop a system of morality divorced from an awareness of, . . . an understanding of one's environment—one's physical, natural environment. . . . This is, I believe an ancient and profound insight: it implies, for example, that moral systems cannot be developed merely in the context of human relationship. . . . Moral systems must account, not merely for the relationship between humans and humans, but for the interrelationship between humans and nature.

He talked on the meaning of the biblical word *shalom*, usually translated 'peace,' but having a wider sense. He goes on to describe

one form of this, Ma'at, from the religious teaching of ancient
Egypt. "First Ma'at means universal order, that is to say that the
world of Nature, the immediate world that we perceive, and the
entire universe is characterized by a certain order, or harmony.
. . . Second Ma'at means social order: it is the order which should
govern or characterize a state; in ancient Egypt the Pharaoh, who
was the patron of Ma'at. It was his responsibility as a ruler to
govern his state according to certain principles of morality, so that
his state, in conjunction with the environment in which it was set
should also be characterized by a certain harmony. Third, Ma'at
means personal or individual truth or integrity. The social harmony of the state, the harmony of the environment, or nature,
must also be perceived in the life of an individual human being. . . ."

This is also the concept of *shalom*, not just cessation of war,
but harmony—man and animals at peace with each other. God
sets before us life and death, good and evil. He commands us to
live in harmony with one another and with nature. We choose to
obey or disobey, to fight or cooperate.

In ecology the nitrogen cycle has three factors: first, the
producers, the plants that produce food from the sun and nutrients
in the soil; second, the consumers, the animals that consume
plants or other animals; third, the decomposers, the bacteria and
fungi that transform dead matter and animal waste in the soil into
the mineral nutrients the plants use again to produce food. But
economics neglects this third factor. It talks only of producers
and consumers and the money, goods, and labor passing between
them. We have been constantly extracting raw materials from the
land and not putting them back.

God does not waste these resources; all decayed matter returns
to the soil to be used. He can even make evil work towards good,
as He did at the Crucifixion. Here on earth Jesus walked and
talked with men, subject to hunger, thirst, humiliation, and death.
"He was despised and rejected of men." He did the work of a
slave when He washed His disciples' feet. But His death became
the source of life, and the Cross which was despised became a
sign of glory. As Paul said, "The things that are despised did God

choose" (I Col. 1:28). So we should not despise the humble little bacteria in the soil doing the work God has ordained in turning death into a source of life. "Except a grain of wheat fall into the ground and die, it has no life." And we should not despise the garbage collector, the scrap-metal merchant, or the recycler. We should give them golden uniforms, for they do a vital work. Our attitude of contempt for old, worn-out things has led us to throwing old iron on the scrap heap to rust instead of recycling it. Now, when metal is getting scarcer, we are beginning to realize our mistake. The recyclers are very important people; so are the repair men and others who help us to avoid waste.

But what of the consumers? What use are they if they just consume? In nature they are the animals, and animals have consciousness. They can enjoy life, and God wants us to enjoy life. In human economics, most people are producers as well as consumers. It is our consumption that gives us the energy to not only do the work of producing material goods, but also the creative and spiritual work to the glory of God.

We often think of things thus in pairs: light and darkness, up and down, man and woman, peace and war, old and young, truth and falsehood. But it is important to recognize a fundamental difference between these types of pairs. Life and death are real opposites: they are going in opposite directions. Likewise good and evil; they have different objectives. But old and young are not going in opposite directions. They can cooperate and live in harmony. Darkness is negative, an absence of light, and therefore its true opposite. But male and female, freedom and discipline, individuality and sociality are pairs that can balance each other and work together. This harmony is typified by the swing of the pendulum or the up and down of a wave or see-saw. With the right swing of the pendulum, we get some freedom, some discipline. But if the pendulum swings to an extreme, the balance is upset and you get violence, an extreme reaction. Freedom becomes each man for himself, leading to chaos, and then dictatorship results in reaction. If there is no energy input, the wave dies down, the pendulum stops, discipline becomes rigid, there is no movement, and spiritual death occurs.

When there is a lack of balance in any of these pairs—if the male is too dominant or individuality overstressed at the expense of sociality—you get either rigidity, with no movement, or chaos. Masefield's[2] description of a cyclone sea typifies this:

> In their experience they had known the power of storms to be associated with order. They had seen the march of big seas coming like ranges of downland, greyback after greyback, sometimes two miles long, well-aligned, moving to the wind, curling in one direction, slipping under the curlings in one direction, and following each other in succession with an arranged space between. . . . Now they looked upon a water that was not only defiled but had gone mad.
>
> There was no kind of order in it, but every kind of devilry. It was (as Dick judged) not so big as the ordered "greyback" sea of the Western Ocean or Cape Horn. It did not give him any sensation or impression of majesty, nor of power, but it seemed to him to be evil cast loose to do what it would; not big determined evil, but limitless hordes of selfish evils, "little devils that fight for themselves," too devilish to agree even about evil, but determined each to rend his neighbour, even if it rent himself.
>
> The thing which impressed Dick most was that it was a shapeless sea. It looked like a revolution. It was a succession of points, teeth and pyramids, coming up confusedly in jags and tatters, butting and boiling into each other, collapsing and spouting. It was as though some devilry had kept all these jags of water under the surface till they had gone mad, and that then they had burst out choking to bite their neighbour and die.

Why do the orderly waves give the impression of majesty and the disorderly jags the impression of evil? Such chaos must lead eventually to entropy, for one energy defeats the other. This symbolizes the waste of war. The ordered waves represent Beauty, Truth, and Love. Gentle curves are beautiful; music and poetry have their rhythm. Truth is the balancing of the equation, the just weighing of the evidence, yet not static. Love is the harmony of two people on the see-saw of life, the differences working together making a whole team.

Jesus showed this balance in His life here: He avoided the rigid attitude of the Pharisees, and the licenciousness of the Herodians. He ate and drank with "publicans and sinners," but did not sin. He taught the absolute opposition between life and death, good and evil.

Competition in the market is meant to be a system of checks and balances that prevents any one producer from getting into a position where he can influence price. Theoretically, market price brings supply and demand into equilibrium so that each producer can sell all that he has at that price. In fact, of course, it is impossible to keep perfect equilibrium and producers usually cannot sell all they have, so they are constantly fighting each other for a bigger share of the market.

It was a mistake to call the ideal "competition": it should be called "demopoly," the system for democracy, the opposite of monopoly. For competition, to most people, means winning over other people, becoming the champion, and that leads to monopoly. This competitive attitude is dominant in our society and we should not encourage it by depicting it as an ideal, nor should we teach it in school. It will eventually lead to either monopoly, dictatorship, and rigid bureaucracy, or to strikes, conflict, bankruptcies, revolution, and chaos. Those are the two extremes we want to avoid. A little competition gives spice to life, but too much spice is a mistake. Cooperation is more important, as Archbishop Temple[3] showed in the following passage:

> At every stage there is co-operation of the three factors—Capital, Management, and Labour. On the day that the co-operation stops, the industry stops. Industry *is* co-operation for public service. If, then, the people who are engaged in it work as if it were competition for private profit, of course it goes wrong. But our thought must be concrete, not abstract. Competition and Co-operation are logical opposites, but they are not incompatibles. Consider a game of football. . . . Inside each team, every player may be competing against all the rest to be the best co-operator in competing against the other team for the co-operative fun of the game. Co-operation and Competition may be inextricably intertwined. But it makes all the

difference which is uppermost—which exercises a check upon the other. If you have the co-operative spirit uppermost, you have good sportsmen, who would rather be beaten in a good game than win in a bad one; but if the competitive spirit is uppermost, you have men who play only to win, and will do any dirty trick that the referee will let them. So in industry our need is a full and frank recognition that industry is in its own nature fundamentally co-operative, so that all competition within it is kept in check by the co-operative spirit and purpose.

We need to recover the ideal of having fun in games and enjoying our work in the market. We need harmony between employer and employee, between producer and consumer, instead of all this antagonism. How can a company thrive without cooperation in its own ranks?

Communism overstresses state control, leading to bureaucracy and rigidity. Capitalism overstresses individualism. This led to chaos in the thirties, so it is now tending to bureaucracy like communism, and to oligopoly—the rule of the big corporation in alliance with the state, as Galbraith describes so well in *Economics and the Public Purpose.*

We should try to cultivate a free market attitude in which all want to maintain a reasonable standard of living *like* their fellows, not *above* them, with a little spice of competition to keep everyone on their toes, but not as much as in this grim rat race. Keeping up with the Joneses is all right so long as the Joneses don't keep trying to get above others. This is really a more natural attitude, seen among people who are closer to nature. We think our attitude is natural, but in reality it has usually been taught. Some children deliberately clamp down on themselves to avoid being far ahead of others; they want to be like their peers, not separate from them. We should cultivate cooperation in school rather than competition, and have children work in teams in schoolwork as well as in play.

Co-operation and Competition among Primitive Peoples[4] shows that many successful societies—Iroquois, Samoans, Zuni, and Maori—stressed cooperation rather than competition, and had satisfactory standards of living, whereas in competitive societies there seems to have been more stress. B. S. Quain writes in it that:

> The ideal structure of Iroquois society, as it was expressed in political theory, reflected the attitudes of women, who during their entire life span were never strongly tempted into individualistic activities. Only feminine activities, which were directed toward cooperative ends and usually organized along kin lines, coincided with the cooperative and pacific principles upon which the League was built.

Systems analysis shows that effective systems have built-in feedback controls that keep the system in a steady state and curb excessive growth or other disruptive behavior. The birth rate of most animals is so high that if it were not curbed, the earth would soon be overpopulated. For populations increase exponentially, that is doubling and doubling again. So the increase is very gradual at first, then it skyrockets. But if rabbits overpopulate, for example, foxes have a plentiful supply of food, so they increase in number too, while the grass supply is decreased by overeating. The rabbit population is thereby decreased again and balance is restored. The pure, free, competitive market is supposed to operate in a similar way. Competition between producers should keep prices down and prevent either over- or underproduction, for if anyone charges a higher price than others, no one will buy from him. At the same time, since no producer can continue to supply for less than cost price (including the normal return to him for his work), price cannot go below cost.

This would naturally lead to a steady-state economy, as balance occurs in nature, with the same amount always being produced at the lowest price with maximum efficiency and no economic profits (that is, above normal returns). But our economic system demands continual growth in the sense of increased quantity. This is contrary to the balanced principle of natural systems. Human populations can only increase at the expense of other species, and we not only increase in population exponentially but also try to increase the amount each person consumes. There is here a basic contradiction in our economic system, since the ideal would lead to a steady state, but economists reject that.

We must here consider the difference between natural growth and mere increase in quantity. All living things grow, but they don't just go on growing bigger. When they get to optimum size they stop, and their growth takes the form of change: increase in strength, or the production of fruit, for example.

In human terms, this should resolve into growth in mental and spiritual qualities. It is very important to understand a basic difference between mental and material growth. The concept is very simple and can be understood by a child. If you have two bananas and you give one to someone else, you have one less. But if you have two ideas in your head and you give one to some-one else, how many ideas do you have left? This demonstrates how continual growth is possible in mental and spiritual matters, where it is not possible in material things, because we live in a finite world.

Now capital, as we have seen, is basically mental, the knowl-edge of how to make and use tools, and to organize our work to increase production. We have tended to think too much of the capital goods, machines, roads, buildings, and money, which are material. When passed on from father to son, goods tend to ac-cumulate in the hands of a few, and the process continues till there is a monopoly of power. But if the principle of sharing abundant knowledge is accepted, as it is in our public school system, then economic democracy is possible. One of the principles of the pure, free, competitive market is supposed to be complete knowledge of the market and of the technology. So let us really open up and share our technology, instead of trying to keep it secret.

So spiritual energy ascending in sacrifice, and mental capital, which does not deteriorate, give us our true "treasure in Heaven," the luxuries we can enjoy with an easy conscience. The Father has provided all we need to furnish our daily bread, all the neces-sities of which He knows we have need. The Son showed us in His life here the true values "not be ministered unto, but to minister" (that is, to serve), and that we should not despise the poor, the small, or the old. The Holy Spirit is the Spirit of Power and Love. He inspires us to create, He teaches us to pray and praise, and of that there need be no end. Our objective in economic life should be, not to make more money, but to use the material things God provides to His Glory and the joy of the rest of mankind.

5

Rich and Poor

Poor people who have to spend twelve hours a day doing physical labor or who are denied the food and tools to enable them to do creative work may be prevented from producing to the glory of God. So also may rich men who spend all their time making money, and well-paid assembly line workers whose creativity is dulled. They are like obese people to whom food, through excess, has become a curse rather than a blessing. When fat people eat more than their share and die of heart failure while poor people have less than their share and die of starvation, both would be better off with a more equal distribution.

Economics does not think of distribution from this point of view, but only in terms of wages, interest, rent, and profit, which are considered chiefly as incentives to work or to lend. Government is supposed to make some attempt at equalization by taxing income, but it doesn't have much effect.

One result of better distribution that has been observed, but has not been taught or practiced enough, is that when workers are paid more, they buy more and so they encourage production. Now, mass production is not useful if luxury goods are produced for a few rich people; it must be aimed at ordinary workers. It is useless unless workers have enough money to buy more than just their basic necessities. Since we started to pay skilled workers more, our economy has flourished, but now we are getting to the point of diminishing utility and have to spend vast sums on advertising to get these richer people to buy junk goods. We would do better to see that the poor, here and in developing countries, get more money so that they can buy the goods they really want. And we should produce what they want, not just what we want to sell. The harm done by overadvertising infant formulas is well documented. But there are many other things that companies, in order to make profit, persuade poor people to buy to their disadvantage.

WAGE DIFFERENTIALS

Is it right that when the minimum wage is $3.50, a plumber should get four times that? The difference is too great. I hear that in Japan a manager usually gets about four times what his average worker gets, while here the manager gets ten times. Why can't we reduce the difference to the Japanese level? The answer is apparently that we can't get managers unless we offer colossal salaries because the strain of their work is so great. What we have to do then is to reduce the strain. But I don't think an electrician experiences four times as much strain as a street cleaner. The rich of today are not just the top 5 percent, they are the skilled workers; only the below average are poor.

THE RICH

What does the Bible say about the rich and the poor? In the Old Testament, riches are sometimes regarded as a blessing from God. "The Lord had greatly blessed my master and made him a rich man. He has given him flocks of sheep and goats, cattle, silver, gold, male and female slaves, camels, and donkeys" (Gen. 24:35). But this is at the beginning of the Bible, among nomadic people; later they are regarded as accursed. "You are doomed! You buy more houses and fields to add to those you already have. Soon there will be no place for anyone else to live, and you alone

will live in the land" (Isa. 5:8). "How terrible it will be for you
that stretch out on your luxurious couches, feasting on veal and
lamb!" (Amos 6:4). But this is chiefly when riches have been
obtained by exploitation or dishonesty, and when they lead to
idleness and drunkenness. In Proverbs, a moderated idea of
enough but not too much is shown to be best: ". . . and let me be
neither rich nor poor. So give me only as much food as I need"
(Prov. 30:8).

The New Testament is even more emphatic. Jesus had aston-
ishing things to say of the rich: "It is easier for a camel to go
through the eye of a needle than for a rich man to enter the
Kingdom of Heaven" (Matt. 19:24). The disciples were aston-
ished at this saying. In the accounts of the Beatitudes, in both
Matthew and Luke, it is stressed that though the multitude had
been there, He was addressing the disciples, and to them He said,
"Woe unto you who are full now, for you shall hunger" (Luke
6:24-25). In the parable of Lazarus and the rich man, it doesn't
say that Lazarus was good and Dives bad. The reason Abraham
gives for Lazarus being with him while Dives was suffering in
Hades is that on earth Lazarus had suffered and Dives had had an
easy life. Jesus said to His disciples, "Sell your possessions and
give alms" (Luke 12:33). And to the rich young ruler He said,
"Sell all that you have and give to the poor." All these sayings
show plainly that He taught that to be rich was undesirable and
even spiritually dangerous. "You cannot serve God and Mammon
(wealth)," He said, but so many Christians today try to do just
that.

THE POOR

The poor are permitted to glean. "When you harvest your
fields, do not cut the grain at the edges of the fields, and do not
go back to cut the heads of grain that were left; leave them for
the poor people and foreigners. The Lord is your God" (Lev.
23:22). They must be helped. "If a fellow Israelite living near

you becomes poor and cannot support himself, you must provide for him as you would for a hired man, so that he can continue to live near you" (Lev. 25:35). The expression "the poor" is often used to describe the good, humble people who are oppressed by others.

And what did Jesus say of the poor? He came to earth as a poor man, born in a barn, worked as a carpenter, and walked the roads of Galilee with a few fishermen friends. He came "to preach good news to the poor" (Luke 4:18). He fed them and He healed them. He said to His disciples, "Blessed are *you* poor, for yours is the Kingdom of Heaven." These disciples had given up material things for His sake and He said, "Truly I say to you, there is no one who has left house or brothers or sisters or mother or father or children or lands, for my sake and for the gospel, who will not receive a hundredfold now in this time, houses and brothers and sisters and mothers and children and lands, with persecutions, and in the age to come eternal life" (Mark 10:29-30). Some people seem to think this means that after they have committed themselves to Jesus they will then become rich, but that is to consider only the words "lands" and "houses," not "children." But if you also have 100 times the number of mothers and children to care for, you will need 100 houses! Surely it is plain that this means all fellow Christians will be your family. They will help to provide for your needs, and you will help to provide for theirs.

THE BEATITUDES

Some people get confused because of the difference between the Beatitudes recorded by Matthew and those recorded by Luke. Personally, I think Jesus said the words recorded by Luke first, "Blessed are you poor, for yours is the Kingdom of God. Blessed are you that hunger now, for you shall be satisfied. But woe to you that are rich, for you have received your consolation. Woe to you that are full now, for you shall hunger" (Luke 6:20-21,

24-25). Then he probably did as many preachers do; He preached
again on the same theme, but expanded on it. He then used the
words "poor in spirit" instead of just "poor" as in Luke's version,
to explain that He didn't mean the mere absence of wealth. The
words "poor in spirit" trouble some people as they sound like
"poor-spirited," and Jesus cannot have meant that the poor-
spirited are blessed, nor that people are happy because they don't
have spiritual treasure. The New English Bible has inserted the
words "know they are" in front, but Jesus did not say that, and
it is wrong to put words into His mouth that He did not say. However, the word *spirit* can mean attitude or disposition, as in
Romans 8:15, where a spirit of bondage leading to fear is contrasted with a spirit of adoption. When we talk of obeying the letter
of the law and not the spirit, we mean that someone is not fulfilling the intention of the law, and Jesus taught frequently that
it is the attitude and intention that counts. "Whoever hates his
brother is a murderer." So the one who hates his riches is poor
in spirit, and the poor man who covets riches is not, nor was
the medieval monk who made a vow of poverty and then lived in
ease in a rich abbey. Perhaps the best modern expression of this
poverty in spirit is "voluntary simplicity."

This does not mean that God wants His people to starve. True,
the word for "the poor" here means the destitute, the beggars, but
many Christians who have become "beggars for Christ" and lived
on faith have been filled. For the second beatitude is "Blessed
are you who are hungry now, for you will be filled." Jesus told
us not to be anxious about what we are to eat or wear, for our
Father "knows that you have need of these things." But He
promises necessities, not luxuries.

Nor does it mean that the rich can ignore the suffering of the
hungry on the grounds that they are more blessed than they are.
This is a hypocritical attitude because, if the rich really believed
that, they would sell their possessions and give to the poor in
order to join the ranks of the blessed themselves. It is this attitude
that has turned some sincere people away from Christ's teaching
on poverty. But the way in which the hungry will be filled is by

the rich brethren sharing with the poor. Communism tells the poor to take from the rich: Christianity tells the rich to give to the poor.

THE FAMILY OF GOD

This does not mean that the rich should stay rich and just give little bits to the poor. Jesus said, "Sell your possessions and give to the poor." The rich have to put themselves in the category of the family on a minimum wage, or at least accept salary cuts. So often we hear demands that ordinary workers should reduce their wage demands, but at the same time we hear of huge increases in profits and in salaries to top public officials. As well as a minimum wage, we need a maximum, and then we should try to squeeze these together, gradually raising one and lowering the other. Those who advocate a steady-state economy instead of constant accelera- tion say this will be necessary anyway, because the main reason for the demand for a "larger pie" is that the rich don't want to give up their excessive share of the pie. Trade unions of highly paid skilled workers also don't want to give up their "historic differential," so they are rich, while unskilled workers are poor and despised. Unions should ask for "across the board" increases instead of percent increases.

In regard to the Third World, we should see to it that workers who work hard providing us with cheap sugar and bananas should receive a living wage. For all of us are rich compared to them. We spend comparatively little of our incomes on food and could well afford to pay more! Those who can't are our poor and should receive a higher wage also. Let us have justice not charity here.

The Church must now start to face up to what Jesus said about the rich and the poor. Sincere Christians are beginning to think more and practice voluntary simplicity. Let us all really try to follow Jesus. We are His Body. Should one part of the Body be obese, while the other part starves? In healthy people the blood takes nourishment to all parts of the body. The members of the family of God must share with each other.

STATUS

Our economic system is strongly affected by the concept of status. By teaching competition we have taught people to try to get on top. But we forget that every time a person gets on top, he is pushing someone else beneath; only a few can get on top, so the majority are bound to fail. And by assuming, as some people do, that everyone has the opportunity to improve their status, we can blame the failure to do so on laziness or stupidity, though in fact there is not equal opportunity for all.

In some simpler cooperative societies, like those of the Iroquois or Samoans, status does not have to be fought for, it comes automatically, perhaps through age or inheritance. The king or chief is not resented because he represents the entire tribe; his status is therefore the status of the whole tribe. His advisers are usually the elders, who have status because of their age, so all men can hope to achieve status automatically without fighting for it.

We tend to think this hereditary status wrong, but is it any worse than fighting each other for it? In *Prime Time*,[1] Mr. Freeman, retired chairman of the board of the First National Bank of Chicago, said: "Business is so damned competitive! The head of a business is really competing with everybody all the time, not only with his competitors. You're competing with your friends in other businesses, your dearest friends. It influences your life tremendously. And not necessarily in a good way. It tends to make business friendships not quite friendships." So he sacrificed real friendships and, he said earlier, that he had sacrificed closeness with his children. He quoted a business friend who said, "There's nobody in town who really likes me. From now on I'm going to lead my life to be liked." But it was too late to change and "he died an unhappy man, with great tension between himself and the children."

Does competition necessarily lead to efficiency? If it's a case of no holds barred, get to the top by any dirty trick, then it doesn't. And anyway, even in our North American society, status is partly hereditary. Most of our elite are from wealthy families.

Those whose status is due to birth cannot rightly blame the lower classes for their lower position, and they have no right to despise them, though they often do. What is so bad about our system is that the poor are despised, and blamed for their condition. But, as teachers know well, the children of the poor do not have an equal opportunity. They start with a handicap.

In the great civilizations of the past, there was usually a pyramidal structure of status and wealth. This results in the majority being at the bottom. As long as these poor people were not starving or actively ill-treated, they had satisfactory status because they were the majority. Most people don't want to be different; they want to be like the others around them. Poverty doesn't matter so much if it is not extreme and everyone is in the same boat.

But in our North American society, the poor are the unemployed and their families, who are in a minority, and are therefore despised. The majority are reasonably well-off and can maintain the accepted standard of living, and they despise those who don't live up to the standard. It is this contempt for the poor that is so bad and basically unchristian. What is required is for everyone to have a recognized position in society, not based on higher or lower concepts, but on the intrinsic importance of that position to the total society.

We need to rethink the whole question of status from a Christian point of view.

The Church teaches that the Three Persons of the Trinity, Father, Son and Holy Spirit, are equal. Yet Paul said, "The head of every man is Christ, the head of a woman is her husband, and the head of Christ is God" (1 Cor. 11:3). Is Jesus equal or subordinate to the Father? Is a woman equal or subordinate to her husband? Jesus obeyed the Father. He was "obedient even unto death." He said, "Not my will, but Thine." Moreover, a son was definitely thought of in those days as subordinate to his father. Yet John says that Jesus "called God his Father, making himself equal to God" (John 5:18). How can we explain this?

I think our lack of understanding comes because we accept the arrogant attitude of so many of our top people. Who is more important, the architect or the builder? Is the architect justified in saying that he is better than a builder? Is it not truer to say that they have different functions, but are equally important? The Father sends out His Word, He gives commands, He makes the laws of the universe, He plans the salvation of Mankind. The Son carries out these commands in voluntary, loving obedience to the Plan, knowing it is a good Plan, just as a good musician obeys the music. But the Head who plans and the Body who performs are equally important.

We have made the grave mistake of assuming that he who gives orders is better than he who obeys them. But the obedience of the Son is not degradation, it is His Glory. It is the humble who are most praised in the Bible, not the proud. We need to return to a truly Christian teaching on humility. The word comes from *humus,* 'the ground, the soil'. It involves walking on the earth side by side with the unemployed, with the single mother on welfare, with the cleaning woman, the Indian, and any others whom society tends to despise. This is the status that Jesus sought and that his followers should seek. And when we do so the Carpenter of Nazareth walks beside us.

ST. FRANCIS OF ASSISI

We should reread the life of St. Francis, and though we would not need to go to the extremes he sometimes went to, we have much to learn from his wholehearted attempt to imitate the lifestyle of Jesus. Mrs. Oliphant, in her biography of him, wrote,

> In the ardour of love and self-abandonment he was fain to do a little more than was asked of him. Poverty was his bride. He loved her for herself. It was his pleasure to be destitute—to starve if God pleased, yet to feel the certainty that he should not starve, neither he nor his brethren, because God cared for them. But this beautiful excess of devotion is a thing which but one individual, here and there, can feel.[2]

Some people think his ideal wrong, because he didn't do

productive work. But preaching and healing is work, and he said, "I desire that all my brethren should labor at useful occupations, that we may be less of a burden to the people. . . . Those who cannot work, let them learn to work."

But one of the chief features of Francis' character was his cheerfulness. Mrs. Oliphant wrote, "When some doubting soul questioned him how it was that he himself, amid so many distractions, preserved his serenity and lightheartedness, Francis replied, 'Sometimes my sins are very bitter to me, sometimes the devil attempts to fill me with a sadness which leads to indifference and sleep; for my joy is a vexation to him. . . . But when I am tempted to sadness and slothfulness, I look at the cheerfulness of my companion, and, seeing his spiritual joy and happiness, I shake off the temptation and the idle sorrow, and am full of joy within and gaiety without.' Such was his version of what a life should be which was led in hunger, and cold, and nakedness, far from every human consolation, for the love of God." Today there seems to be such a lack of this joy within.

But when ordinary people with dependents and responsibilities, which made it impossible for them to embrace absolute poverty, wanted to follow Francis, he started for them the Third Order. "He knew that the world must still go on and fulfill its everyday labours, whatever might be suggested by the enthusiasm of the moment. . . . 'Remain in your homes,' he said, 'and I will find for you a way of serving God.' "[3]

I think the Church needs something like this now. Christians seem to fall often into the error of regarding the following of Christ as work for an elite—ministers, monastic orders, missionaries, and others—and not for all members of His body. But He never taught that. Only certain people were told to sell *all* their possessions; Zachaeus gave half of his goods; Martha, Mary, and Lazarus continued to live at home, but were His friends; And Jesus Himself set an example of ordinary life when He worked as a village carpenter. But He had given up His throne and His crown to do it. What shall we give up?

6

Capitalism and Free Enterprise

Most people think that capitalism and free enterprise are the same, but if we think more deeply about these words we can see a difference. Capitalism comes from the word *capital* and is usually thought of as starting with the Industrial Revolution, though some place the start as the previous amassing of financial capital aided by the banking system. It is therefore associated with big money and industry; and the growth of capitalism has involved the control of these in the hands of a few powerful people.

Free enterprise should mean that anyone is free to start their own enterprise if they wish, to own their own business as entrepreneurs; that is, all should have the chance to become owner-managers. The word is therefore particularly applicable to small businesses and farming. The conventional "pure, free, competitive market" of the economists requires this sort of business. But freedom to run this sort of business must involve more than mere legal permission to do so. It must include economic possibility. Nowadays capitalism has increased—the multinational corporations are the epitome of it—but free enterprise has decreased.

CAPITALISM AND COMMUNISM

People think of capitalism and communism as opposites. In fact they are in many ways very similar and are getting more so:

1. They are both materialistic and ignore spiritual values. Communism is actively against religion; capitalism merely ignores it, but by teaching materialism it has undermined the Church's values and given people another god, the almighty dollar.

2. Both have the objective of producing more and more, and so favor industrialization and big plants in a big way.

3. This leads to concentration of power and the rule of an elite—rich businessmen in one, communist leaders in the other.

4. Both assume that the majority of people will not own much land or capital, and so will have to be employed by the controllers of it, working for money, rather than producing their own necessities.

5. This puts employer and employee in different classes. Marxists preach class warfare as a principle; capitalism has bred antagonism between the classes by the self-interested, competitive attitude, which compels employers to pay as little as possible and workers to demand as much as possible.

6. Both are tending towards state capitalism—that is, big corporations in alliance with the state. The corporations are moving into Russia and China; they are already in positions of great power in the Latin American dictatorships and, since the producers are being bought out by the financiers, it is the latter who gain power.

7. They both profess to be democratic, but the amount of freedom enjoyed by the people varies. If we compare the USA and USSR, the capitalist country seems to have more freedom. But if we compare Argentina with Yugoslavia, we should probably find that there was more freedom in the communist country. It doesn't depend on the economic system, but on the government. There are capitalist dictatorships also; we fought against one in the Second World War.

CAPITALIST PRINCIPLES

The antireligious principles of communism are well known

but, since capitalism began in Christian countries, Christians should reconsider its basic principles.

Ayn Rand[1] wrote, "Capitalism and altruism are incompatible." Altruism is defined as "unselfishness; unselfish devotion to the interests and welfare of others." So in capitalism, according to Rand, we would be selfish. But is this a correct assumption about capitalism? It is defined as, "an economic system of private ownership of property; production of goods for profit; and the institution of bank credit."[2] *Encyclopedia Brittanica* also stresses the essential part of bank credit in it, that it is for profit, and concerns the ownership of the means of production. An economics text[3] gives its characteristics as "private property, freedom of enterprise and choice, self-interest as a motivating force, competition, and reliance on a price system"; with in addition, "the use of advanced technology and large amounts of capital goods, specialization, and the use of money." It was the capital lent by banks and the great use of capital goods that gave it the name "capitalism."

1. *The banking system* is based on the custom of depositing money in a bank but not drawing it out immediately. The banks can therefore lend some of that money to others and charge them interest. In the Old Testament, Jews were forbidden to charge interest to fellow Jews; and for several centuries the Christian Church also forbade the charging of interest.

2. *Profit maximization* means making as much money as possible, over and above a fair return for your labor and capital. Jesus said, "Lay not up for yourselves treasures on earth." The principle of profit making is so basic that Milton Friedman argues that the sole duty of a company is to make profits for its shareholders; management has no other business, so social responsibility is ruled out. But this extreme view is, in a sense, contradictory, as it assumes that managers will put the interest of the firm above their own self-interest.

3. *Individualism and self-interest*. Adam Smith,[4] the first great economist, said that a man who works on the principle of self-interest "is in this, as in many other cases, led by an invisible hand to promote an end which is no part of his intention. . . . By pursuing his own interest he frequently promotes that of society

more effectually than when he really intends to promote it." This saying seems to have become the chief text of the capitalist bible! But Jesus said, "Deny yourself," "Take up your cross daily," and "Love your neighbour as yourself." That last command assumes that people naturally have self-interest, but what needs to be taught is altruism and control of the self-interest, not encouraging it as capitalism does. In this respect I find that the Church has gone along too much with the ideas of capitalism and psychology. So often when I point to Jesus' saying, "Deny yourself," I hear Christians arguing against it, not on the basis of Scripture, but psychologically, interpreting the saying "Love your neighbour as yourself" as if it involved a third commandment, "Love yourself." In fact, some Christians make that the First Commandment, but Christ said the first was to Love God. The biblical assumption (as expressed in Eph. 5:29) is that loving yourself is certainly natural, but is nowhere encouraged, and should be used to teach altruism. A little child is naturally egoistic. He doesn't have to be taught that, he has to be taught to think of others. Even those who say they hate themselves want themselves to succeed and be better, which is a form of self love, for we want those we love to achieve their greatest potential; whereas if we hate someone, we don't want them to succeed. It wouldn't be so bad if capitalism taught self-interest *and* community or family interest, but it doesn't; it teaches *only* self-interest and duty to the company as motives.

This does not mean, however, that we go to the opposite extreme of communism and deny the importance of the individual. It is more that we should think of the individuality of others. Jesus dealt with people as individuals, but He did not encourage them to be selfish. If Tom, Mary, and Carol each turn in on themselves and say, "I'm wonderful," they may feel proud of themselves, but they may not be liked by others. But if Tom says to Carol and Mary, and Mary says to Tom and Carol, "You're wonderful," then they will all get a moral boost that will last, and friendship also.

4.   *The free market.* Adam Smith was more reasonable than his followers have become. His concept of the free market is similar in some ways to the picture of nature's ecological balance

and could work in a small system. He was a moral philosopher, so when he talked of the Invisible Hand impelling man's self-interest to work for the good of society, he probably thought of this as God's Hand. But though we know that God can turn evil to work for good, He does not thereby condone evil. In the animal world He has ordained that the struggle for survival leads to a balance in nature and to the survival of the fittest.

But humans permit their less fit to survive; even in old days they gave to beggars. Sometimes the less fit may turn out to be the ones who excel in intellect, art, or the spiritual qualities that we value.

Anyway, we cannot run our lives as the plants and animals do, in little ecosystems, for several reasons. One is that we do not act as much on instinct as animals do, but according to culture and reason. Animals do not strive to get more possessions than they need, but man looks to the future and hoards. Animals fight for power, but in a limited way; whereas man can accumulate power. The balance of the free market, though a good ideal, is upset by cutthroat competition, collusion, accumulation of power and money, so that frequently it does not work out for the good of society. However, it can and should be improved?

5. *Competition* is a part of the economist's model of the free market. Heilbroner[5] writes that "it provides the regulator that 'supervises' the orderly working of the market. It does so because economic competition, unlike the competition for prizes outside economic life, is not a single contest, but a continuing process—a race in which the runners never win, but must go on endlessly trying to stay in front to avoid the penalties of falling behind. . . . For the competitive marketplace is not only where the clash of interest between buyer and seller is worked out by the opposition of supply and demand, but also where buyers contend against buyers and sellers against sellers."

Notice especially in this passage the adversary concepts: "clash of interest," "sellers against sellers," and the grim prospect of a race that you cannot win.

This kind of competition, the opposite of monopoly, should really be given a different name, such as *demopoly*, because it is not what we usually mean by competition. There is a basic contradiction between this form of competition, where all stay about equal, and competition as rivalry, where one tries to defeat the others and come out on top with a monopoly. This is really more characteristic of our economic system, and has led to the destruction of many small firms and their takeover by the big corporations.

This adversary attitude between firm and rival firm, between consumer and producer, between employers and workers is also contrary to Christian principles. The only real fight Christians are involved in is that between good and evil. We cannot say "Consumers are good and producers are bad." Therefore, there should be no need of conflict here.

THE CAPITALIST RELIGION

How far have Christians accepted these basic principles? John Bennet,[6] in *The Northern Plainsman*, describes attitudes of farmers. He said that throughout American cultural tradition, there are references to the idea that the free-market system is the best in the world and, if left alone, will function perfectly. They think that social inequalities are due to people's personal qualities; some people are lazy, so they are poor. Anyone can get to the top by working hard. People get what they deserve and the poor are just immoral and lazy. Riches are taken as a sign of God's favor, a result of hard work. "God helps those who help themselves" is their motto.

This probably represents fairly well the beliefs of most North Americans. But is it Christian doctrine? I suppose most of these farmers would call themselves Christian, but probably nowadays not many of them go to church regularly. Their belief seems to be composed of items from the Bible, from economists' teachings, from popular sayings, and newspaper articles, all mixed up. Where does the saying, "God helps those who help themselves," come from? Not from the Bible. Does the Bible teach that riches are a sign of God's favor? In the early parts of the Old Testament this is sometimes shown, but in the Psalms, the prophetic writings, and the New Testament they are not; the rich are often shown as bad people.

Is all this even true? Have most rich people really worked harder than the poor? Many got rich by speculation, others inherited wealth. Thurow[7] writes that 50 percent of the very rich inherited wealth, the other 50 percent "accumulate so much and so rapidly that it could not possibly have come through a process of patient saving—and investment at market rates. . . . The winners are lucky rather than smart." Are others poor just because they are lazy? Many people do back-breaking work for twelve hours a day and only get a starvation wage. Even among farmers I don't think the successful ones have always worked harder. Our boom and bust economy favors the farmer who starts off richer, as he can last out the bust and take advantage of the boom, while the poorer farmer has to sell for what he can get, and so grows poorer.

This is not Christianity; it is the Capitalist religion, whose chief god is the almighty dollar, with Mars the god of War, Venus the goddess of sex, Bacchus the god of wine, Santa Claus the god of children, and the national flag the great idol. Dr. Van Dyk[8] in his talk to the Christian Farmers Federation talked of the pagan spirits of individualism, dualism, and natural law, which started in Greece and returned to the Western world at the Renaissance. Since that time all the educated people of Europe have been raised on pagan literature. No wonder the old gods have returned!

Perhaps the most damning indictment of capitalism is made by Keynes in *Essays in Persuasion*: "For at least another hundred years we must pretend to ourselves and to everyone that fair is foul and foul is fair; for foul is useful and fair is not. Avarice and usury and precaution must be our gods for a little longer still. For only they can lead us out of the tunnel of economic necessity into daylight."[9] Christians cannot accept that "avarice and usury must be our gods," nor that only they can lead us into daylight.

But if we put Christian principles first, put altruism before self-interest, cooperation before competition, and cash flow before excess profit, we can return to the free enterprise ideal. A pure free market, based on cash-flow, break-even principles, allowing a reasonable return, would be modeled on the pure competitive model, and would in fact be *more* feasible than the latter, which destroys itself by the drive of self-interest, profit maximization, and the "winning of the competition" by the big corporations. The ideal of many free enterprise economists could be realized *better* if the unchristian elements were absent. "Seek first the Kingdom of God and all these things shall be added."

Informal Economies

CURRENT TRENDS

It is no use just studying economic theories based on nine-teenth-century ideas. We must face the reality of today. The ideal of small entrepreneurs in a free market is not what we see around us. We see these small businesses caught up in the power of the big companies, and the latter growing in power and complexity with mergers and takeovers resulting in conglomerates and multi-national corporations, which can and do fix prices. We see governments taking more and more responsibility for the economic situation, and the people insist that they should be responsible. Whether this actually gives them more power, or whether they have to treat more with these big companies and so get in their power, is debatable. Galbraith points out that[1] "the mature corporation, so far from being separated organically from the state, exists . . . only in intimate association with it." In Crown corporations the profit goes to the state, but they are run like other corporations. Is there any difference, except who gets the profit, between a public utility owned by a municipality and one owned by a private firm?

When the government of Alberta took over Pacific Western Airlines, a local weekly suggested that this was the beginning of "state capitalism." Only a little while before, China had said that the set-up in Russia was not communism but "state capitalism."

Should that make us think? Now China is opening its doors to multinational corporations. This seems to indicate that both conservative and communist governments are moving toward state capitalism and dictatorship. We see this in South America.

DEMOPOLY

But there is an opposite trend and one of the most significant points about it is that nearly all those involved have certain moral and social ideals. They put better conditions for humanity first, with efficiency, industry, and material progress only as some of the possible means of achieving it. They do not think of people as mere consumers or labor as a commodity, but of communities of individuals; hence the stress is on small communities, decentralization, freedom, craftsmanship, friendship and understanding, physical and mental health, sharing things, and aesthetic and religious aspirations.

There are a great variety of groups following this trend. Some are socialist, though not communist; some are old-fashioned conservative. There are decentralists, environmentalists, craftsmen, independent businessmen, community preservation groups, humanitarians, hippies, small farmers, and ethnic and religious groups. Most of them started in a small way, demanding action on some particular issue, but gradually, as they grew, they became aware of other groups with similar ideals. So a network of shared information has sprung up and we have become aware of our common humanity. Capitalism and communism, by overvaluing machines and inanimate objects for consumption, are eroding our humanity. We are being treated as commodities or machines or just numbers and are rebelling against it. It is in small groups and communities of people who know each other that we find our true selves.

Grant Maxwell, in *Attitudes at the Canadian Crossroads,*[2] found that people are longing for life to be more human. He writes, "There is dissatisfaction with our way of life and a recognition that material things don't add up to happiness," but that "only a small minority has systematically set about scaling down consumption, eliminating waste, deepening relationships and otherwise modifying their living patterns." This shows that many are with the new trend mentally, but need to be shown how they can get free and start to practice it.

TRADITIONAL ECONOMIES

Some in this network believe in the principle of self-sufficiency, going back to growing our own food and living more simply. Indeed, when we read of the misery in Third World countries now, it seems that they were better off under the old traditional systems.

There are great varieties of tradition in the economic systems of different countries, but certain generalizations can be made.

1. *Land*. Commonly, each family has a plot of land on which to grow food, but this land is not usually owned outright, it is thought of as belonging to the tribe or village. If a family goes away, it may lose the right to it.

2. *Labor*. In some societies there are traditional ways in which poorer people work for the rich in return for land, protection, food, or money. More often, peasants just work for their families, with most of the work being done by the women. At seed time and harvest everyone may work hard. Leisure is pursued at other times. The attitude is to work when it is necessary, or when something special is desired and must be worked for, but not to do more than is needed for basic necessities and other goods to conform with the customary standard of life.

3. *Capital*. The capital may consist of simple tools and the seed that the family has saved and not eaten. Savings are also in the form of jewelry, though this is not productive capital, and cattle. Some societies have irrigation systems, terraces, roads, and public buildings built with communal labor. In some countries there is a considerable difference between the rich and the poor and accumulation of wealth by the rich in the form of buildings,

jewelry, and money, giving them great power, but it is not often used productively. In other societies the chief of a tribe may have extra stores of food and a bigger house, but these are in a sense held to belong to the tribe, and are used as public money to entertain guests, give feasts, and relieve distress in time of famine. A rich farmer, who accumulates extra food, may invite neighbors to help him build a house or a boat, and then give a feast to them in payment. This is a productive use of capital.

4. *Money and Trade.* Although most of the necessities of life were produced by each family, there is a considerable amount of trade in other things. Sometimes it is barter, but money in different forms has evolved in primitive societies. The big open-air markets in Third World countries are a better example of free-market principles than our stores. Anyone with a surplus product can sell it there. Selling in the streets of a town is also common and open to anyone. Carpenters, tailors, metalworkers, and other craftsmen may make and sell their wares in the open with less restraint than we experience. This is free enterprise, though one would not call it capitalism.

POVERTY

That primitive man's life was "poor, nasty, brutish and short" is not a true generalization. Of course, if a people were forced into the desert or lived in the Arctic, life was difficult and there was much starvation. But many primitive societies satisfied their needs quite well and seldom experienced famine. The Northwest Coast Indians had an abundance of salmon; the Iroquois had good agriculture; the Samoans, Maoris, and many South Sea Islanders had easy lives. They didn't have, or want, the many gadgets we have, but they had more leisure. In hunter-gatherer societies, the work-week may be only 20-25 hours long.

In the Bible, famine is recorded in the times of Joseph and of Elijah, but Canaan was usually "a land flowing with milk and honey." Poverty is more often associated with war, taxes, or exploitation by the rich. In other words, it is man-made, rather than being a basic economic problem. The assumption is that God provides in abundance and there is no need for poverty.

Of course, there have often been famines, but so there are today. Lack of transport to bring food in from a region of surplus was often a cause in old days. Sometimes overpopulation led to overuse of the land, erosion, salination, and so forth. But many societies had simple methods of birth control. The massive over-population of today is, of course, a different matter.

But, people say, there is no starvation in the industrialized countries. Doesn't that show that industrialization is the key? Not necessarily, because if everyone gets as rich and industrialized as the West, to whom shall we sell? At present, we don't have famine because we are rich and can buy food from other countries, but if they take to using their natural resources for themselves, we might starve again, for we import a lot of food from Third World countries. We also depend for food production on vast quantities of oil.

THE INFORMAL ECONOMY

But at one of the workshops at the UN Forum on Habitat, when most people were urging a back-to-the-land movement, Bishop Montefiore from South London asked, "What use is that to my people? They cannot go back to the land. Most of them depend on the auto industry and if that collapses, what is there for them?" And no one had an answer.

But Jane Jacobs in *The Economy of Cities*[3] tells how Los Angeles was saved from depression by small businesses. It was in 1949, when the movie industry was declining and aircraft- and shipbuilding for the war had ceased. "But as it turned out, work and jobs did not decline; they grew. . . . The city's economy had expanded while its exports had been contracting! What was hap-pening, of course, was that Los Angeles was replacing imports at a great rate. The importance of improving balance of trade by reducing imports is seldom mentioned; and small local industries are especially suited to this, as they know what local people want to buy. . . . Much of this new local production work was being done by new local companies or by older ones that were adding new work, and most enterprises, in both categories, were small when they began replacing imports. The new enterprises started in corners of old loft buildings, in Quonset huts, and in backyard garages. But they multiplied swiftly."

A paper by the Vanier Institute of the Family[4] tells of

> volunteers, hunters, fishermen, subsistence farmers, odd-jobbers, artists, craftsmen, and the like . . . who are able to survive not only due to a wide array of earned cash payments and subsidies, but also as a result of their many unpaid self-sustaining economic activities, such as growing food, gathering fuel, building, and repairing buildings and equipment. . . . The hundreds of thousands of people involved in these marginal activities rely upon their many personal abilities to satisfy a *domestic, local or community defined* need whether it be of a resource, production or service nature. The continued existence of our already fragile personal and familial relationships and community networks depends, far more than is currently perceived, upon the vast number of economic activities that constitute the work of such persons in what we will call the Community/Marginal sector.

James Robertson expresses similar ideas in *The Sane Alternative.*[5]

But if each person works alone, this development will not be effective enough. What is needed is, first, the family as a team, the local community working cooperatively, then communication between different communities that have the same way of life.

Arthur Morgan, in *The Community of the Future,*[6] writes, "The time is probably past for small-scale society to live in isolation, whether as to economic life, education, or any other field. The peoples and interests of the world are becoming interdependent. In economic life the feasible alternative to centralized large-scale industry, ruled from the top, is not small units existing in isolation from each other, but rather autonomous small units in some way federated for each other's mutual benefit."

Scott Burns, in his book *Home Inc.*, shows the value of women's work in the home and how the family home is accumulating capital goods. While it is very difficult to assess the value of the household economy, as by its very nature no monetary transactions take place and no figures accrue to the GNP as usually calculated, it is still evident from these studies that Burns quotes in some detail that the household economy is significant. He says,

> America is going to be transformed by nothing more or less than the inevitable maturation and decline of the market economy. The instrument for this powerful change will be the household—the family—revitalized as a powerful and relatively autonomous productive unit. . . . The household is the hero of this book *because it is an economy* and, unlike the market economy, which has shown so much anxiety of late, it is healthy, stable, and growing.[7]

It may seem that these ideas are just little makeshift projects that will have no real effect on the economy but, as Hazel Henderson shows in her chapter on *The Emerging Counter Economy*,[8] these ideas are increasingly being put into practice. We don't want a ready-made economic plan put out by government or big business or economists. We should provide a framework in which these small ideas can grow, thereby arriving at a more natural situation. Above all we should consider whether such systems will lead to a more loving, neighborly life, more in accord with the Christian way of life.

8

Action

Jesus said, "Be doers of the word and not hearers only." The Church should take special action in accordance with His teaching. We must show our love of our neighbor in practice, remembering that he may be the man "who fell among thieves." We must take a stand for justice and freedom.

1. *Freedom.* If we have free enterprise it should be for all, not just for companies or the rich. Everyone should have economic freedom, which involves a certain right to choice, and enough money for this.

People realize that materialism doesn't bring happiness, but they don't know what to do about it. They are caught up in the system; this means they are not free, and especially that they are mentally in bondage. We need a different type of liberation theology here, based on Jesus' saying, "The truth will set you free."

Many people are in bondage to debt. Perhaps Jesus' saying to them will be "Sell all you have and pay your debts." Others suffer from "spending addiction" through credit cards. This must be treated like any other addiction in the AA way, but with demands that people first recognize that it is an addiction. Some are in bondage through social pressure, others through television, others just through apathy or habit, and others are misled by the media and the education system.

The truth—nothing but the truth can set people free. But many people dare not face the truth; to dare it one must have courage, and for courage one must have hope. If there really was no hope for the future, to hide one's head in the sand might be the best thing to do. Those who point out the dangers ahead are often called "doom and gloom" prophets, though in fact most of them are saying, "There is hope *if* you change your ways," whereas those who refuse to listen are the real "doom and gloom" people—they hide their heads because they think there is no hope. W must therefore give them a vision of a viable, socially just structure. And, for the Christian, hope depends on faith in Christ.

2. *Justice.* Justice is constantly taught in the Bible. The Greek word for justice can also be translated as *righteousness.* Are people really treated justly? Do poor people have equal opportunity? The Church must be prepared to fight against injustice wherever it is found. We should visit the law courts, examine the effect of the school system on the poor, and be just in our attitudes by asking ourselves, "If I had been raised like that, would I do the same?"

WHAT CHURCH LEADERS CAN DO

1. Preach on the sins of selfishness, "covetousness which is idolatry," and the biblical teaching on usury.

2. Preach on the positive virtues of sharing, *shalom* as harmony of the whole, the Kingdom of Heaven and its justice, voluntary simplicity as expressed in the saying, "Blessed are the poor," humility as having the right attitude to the poor and being ready to serve them and raise their status.

3. Study *Small is Beautiful, Enough Is Enough, Aid for the Overdeveloped West, Justice Not Charity,* and *The Sane Alternative.* (See also Suggested Reading.)

4. Put these teachings into practice, repent of those sins, worship more simply, don't spend too much on church buildings, elect the poorest people to Church offices, use church buildings for society, get church members to share their knowledge and help each other.

5. Start a land Trust. Members could invest together in land

and put it in the trust of the church to be preserved as agricultural land. It is then rented on long lease to good young farmers who would not be able to start farming otherwise. Specific conditions for the care of the land and animals can be made. Or similar trusts can be started for building houses for disadvantaged people.

ACTION IN FAMILIES

In Jesus' day, with an extended family system, it was probably comparatively easy for a disciple to leave his wife and children in care of other family members. We don't know the precise arrangements that were made, but we can be sure that the promise of providing necessities would apply to them.

Today in this country, where there is usually no such family set-up, it is more difficult in some ways. We realize that many parents do give themselves to a career, but sometimes this is at the expense of their children who are then deprived of the love and care they need. We don't wish to encourage this.

A better concept for a Christian family is that of setting an example of voluntary simplicity in life-style, with a special stress on the voluntary part, which should involve the children, who should be inspired to see this as a challenge and a real way in which they can be doing something to make a better future for all. It is very important that children should be freed from the bondage of television and of riches. You endanger your child's immortal soul if you bring him up to be dependent on riches, for it will then be easier for a camel to go through the eye of a needle than for him to enter the Kingdom of Heaven.

Here are some practical ideas:

1.   Practice the concept that all we have is God's, and teach it to your children in daily life. For example, you may say, "We have room in God's car for someone else, shall we invite So-and-So?"

2. Have regular times of abstinence when you put the money you would spend on food into a collecting box.

3. Befriend a lonely person or a family poorer than you and

encourage your children to invite a friendless child home. That person *is* then Jesus, for He said, "Inasmuch as you have done it to the least of these my brethren you have done it to Me."

4. Encourage the family as an economic unit. Produce your own vegetables and process them, or make clothes, getting your children to help and showing them how they are thereby earning money for the family. But don't pay them, they should be willing to do their bit in return for all they receive. If they insist they ought to be paid, you might suggest that in that case they ought to pay Mum for cooking for them!

5. Be willing to accept a lower paying job, or one of lower status, if that job is intrinsically better and involves real service to mankind. Take the servant attitude as Jesus did. Well-educated people can make do on less, because they know how to handle money more efficiently.

6. Teach children to take care of pets, as the Lord takes care of His "sheep" in Psalm 23.

7. Discourage waste; recycle where possible. Children can get fun out of collecting bottles, paper, etc.

8. Enjoy God.

SHOCK TROOPS

Action for justice and liberation from the bonds of materialism needs shock troops—people with a firm faith and total commitment to God's work. It is worth noting that the command, "Sell all that you have and give to the poor," was addressed to a young man. Probably then he had no dependents and therefore could give himself absolutely to service.

So all young Christians with no dependents should meditate particularly on this story in Mark 10:17-22. Note that it says, "Jesus looking on him *loved* him and said . . ." Most people in this country are rich in comparison with people in the Third World, therefore we must say to ourselves, "We are the rich. What are we going to do about it?"

This total commitment may involve deliberately eschewing

marriage so as to be free to do the Lord's work. Paul's injunctions on virginity should be examined (I Cor. 7:29, 34-35). Note that he enjoins virginity in order that Christians should be able to devote themselves to the work of the Lord because of the urgency of the world situation. This urgency is certainly apparent today. There are others who could commit themselves wholly—widows and retired people on pensions—who no longer need to earn a living, as well as parents whose children are all grown up.

But, such people say, "We've still got to live." Yes, and the promise is that if you are seeking first the Kingdom, God will see that your necessities are supplied. Some people have the strange idea that seeking God's Kingdom involves not working, just praying and meditating all day. That is not Christian teaching, it is more Buddhist. I know of a Christian group doing voluntary social work who find they can take well-paying jobs for a few months and their earnings will do for a year of simple living. Others may be supported by the Church, as will be right when they are doing the Church's work. God will show us what to do. Whatever it may be it should, if possible, be done through a church structure in conjunction with other Christians, and it should be practiced, not just preached.

Examples of these shock troops abound: the ancient monastic orders, the Salvation Army, the Amish and Mennonite settlements, the new intentional communities, as well as many individuals doing their own thing here and there. Perhaps we have a special need for a new order of Franciscans really following the example of Francis of Assisi.

What should their function be? Each one may be called by God to a different vocation. But some will perhaps give a vision of a viable, socially just system; others may teach in their living and ordinary conversation what Christian principles should be; others may just help the poor and the sick in body and mind; others may take a stand for justice.

Will this involve politics? In a sense, yes. If Jesus' actions had not involved politics in some way He would not have been crucified. But He refused to be made a worldly king; He did not tell the poor to take from the rich, but told the rich to give to the poor, which, if they obeyed, would change the power structure. Unfortunately, in the past the Church has often told the poor not to take from the rich, but has omitted to tell the rich to give up their riches. And sometimes where Church leaders and organizations have urged the rich to give, they have nullified their preaching by amassing riches themselves. The money is to be given to the poor, more than to the Church. It is the poor who represent Christ, for He said, "I was hungry and you fed Me." They are His blessed ones for they will be filled. So we should preach to the leaders of capitalism, to the richest in the land, that they should give up their riches and join the ranks of the blessed. Liberation theology should aim at freeing the rich also from their addiction.

CONCLUSION

Bishop Taylor, in *Enough Is Enough*,[1] suggests slogans for Christians:
"The non-violent dominion."
"Joyful resistance movement."
"Refusing to be conned."
"Families for defiance."
"Things don't have to be like this."
These could be made into posters, printed on T-shirts, distributed, and then practiced.

He writes, "We need a thoughtful, convinced minority that will live in such a way as to challenge the cherished beliefs of the consumer society and defy its compulsion. . . . Those are the interests and that the philosophy against which we have to organize our light-hearted revolution. I say light-hearted with deliberation because I am sure that once we begin to take ourselves too seriously we offer our opponent too many hand holds." And I would add that we forget that joy is one of the fruits of the spirit.

The final word in Christian economics is Jesus' saying, "Seek first the Kingdom of Heaven and all these things shall be added." Technologically, there is no problem—we can provide all the basic necessities for all the people of the world. The problems are the greed and selfishness that leads to some taking more than their share, the fear and hatred that causes us to spend so much on armaments, and the apathy that stops us from tackling these sins. These are moral problems and so eminently the responsibility of the Church. Let us preach the Good News to the poor.

Notes

1.

1. H. V. Morton, *In the Steps of the Master* (London: Rich & Cowan, 1934), p. 154.

*2. G. K. Chesterton, *The Everlasting Man* (New York: Doubleday, 1974).

3. Mrs. Oliphant, *Francis of Assisi* (London: Macmillan, 1889), p.123.

4. William Dunbar, "On the Nativity of Christ," *Oxford Book of English Verse* (Oxford: Clarendon Press, 1939), p. 29.

5. Henry Vaughan, "Nature, Man, Eternity," *Oxford Book of English Verse* (Oxford: Clarendon Press, 1939), p. 412.

6. Rudyard Kipling, "Recessional," *Oxford Book of English Verse* (Oxford: Clarendon Press, 1939), p. 1076.

2.

1. Max Weber, *The Protestant Ethic and the Spirit of Capitalism* (Reading, Mass.; Allen & Unwin, Inc., 1930), p. 59.

3.

*1. C. H. Douglas, *Social Credit* (Institute of Economic Democracy, 1979), pp. 49-50.

2. *The New Internationalist*, no. 89 (Oxford: New Internationalist, Ltd., 1980), p. 20.

*3. R. H. Tawney, *Religion and the Rise of Capitalism* (New York: Penguin Books, 1938), p. 104.

4. Ibid., p. 115.

Books in the note section with an asterisk, in addition to the suggested readings that follow, also are recommended.

*5. Charles Carter, *Wealth* (New York: Penguin Books, 1971), pp. 56-57.

4.

1. Peter Craigie, "Ancient Wisdom and Modern Liberty." Speech given at Banff Conference on Man and His Environment, 1978.
2. John Masefield, *Victorious Troy* (Toronto: Macmillan, 1935), p. 207.
3. William Temple, *Christus Veritas* (London: Macmillan, 1939), p. 204.
4. *Co-operation and Competition among Primitive 'Peoples,* ed. Margaret Mead (Gloucester, Mass.: Peter Smith, 1976), pp. 277.

5.

1. Freeman, *Prime Time*
2. Mrs. Oliphant, *Francis of Assisi* (London: Macmillan, 1889), p. 136.
3. Ibid., p. 139.

6.

1. Ayn Rand, *Capitalism: The Unknown Ideal* (New York: New American Library, 1966).
2. *Columbia Viking Encyclopedia,* "Capitalism."
3. R. Boreham, *An Outline of Introductory Economics.*
4. Adam Smith, *The Wealth of Nations,* quoted from George Soule, *Ideas of the Great Economists* (New York: New American Library, 1952), p. 42.
5. Robert Heilbroner, *The Economic Problem* (Englewood Cliffs: Prentice-Hall, 1970), p. 424.
6. John Bennett, *The Northern Plainsman: Adaptive Strategy and Agrarian Life* (Arlington Heights, Ill.: AHM Publishing Corp., 1970).
7. Lester C. Thurow, *The Zero-Sum Society* (New York: Penguin Books, 1981), pp. 172-175.
*8. John Van Dyk, *Of Spirits and Dragons* (Edmonton: Christian Farmers' Federation, 1976).
9. J. M. Keynes, *Essays in Persuasion* (New York: Macmillan, 1972).

7.

*1. J. K. Galbraith, *The New Industrial State* (New York: New American Library, 1971), p. 289.

2. Grant Maxwell, *Attitudes at the Canadian Crossroads* (Ottawa: Vanier Institute of the Family).

*3. Jane Jacobs, *The Economy of Cities* (New York: Random, 1969).

*4. *Seeing Our Economy Whole*. A Public Statement by the Vanier Institute of the Family, Ottawa, 1976, p. 2.

*5. James Robertson, *The Sane Alternative* (7 St. Ann's Villas, London W11 4RU, James Robertson, 1978).

*6. Arthur E. Morgan, *The Community of the Future* (Yellow Springs, Ohio: Community Services, Inc., 1957), p. 101.

*7. Scott Burns, *Home Inc.* (New York: Doubleday, 1975), p. 3.

*8. Hazel Henderson, *Creating Alternative Futures* (Berkly Publishing Corporation, 1978).

8.

*1. John V. Taylor, *Enough is Enough* (London: SCM Press, 1975), pp. 64, 68.

Suggested Reading

Club of Rome Reports, esp. Mesarovic and Pestel, *Mankind at the Turning Point*. New York: Dutton, 1974, and Laslo, *et al.*, *Goals for Mankind* (pub. ditto).

Coady, M. M. *Masters of Their Own Destiny*. New York: Harper & Row. The story of the Antigonish way of adult education through economic cooperation. *The Antigonish Way*. Antigonish, Nova Scotia: St. Francis Xavier University.

Daly, Herman. *Steady State Economics*. San Francisco: W. H. Freeman, 1977.

Goudzwaard, Bob. *Aid for the Overdeveloped West*. Toronto: Wedge Pub. Co., 1975.

Hancock, A. E. *The Road to Monetary Reform*. Raymond, Alberta: Insight Pub. Co., 1978.

Longacre, Doris J. *Living More with Less*. Scottdale, Pa.: Herald Press, 1980.

Sale, Kirkpatrick. *Human Scale*. New York: Cowan, McCann, & Geoghegan, 1980.

Schumacher, E. F. *Small Is Beautiful and Good Work*. New York: Harper & Row, 1979.

Sider, Ronald, J. *Rich Christians in an Age of Hunger*. London: Hodder & Stoughton, 1977.

Solomon, Lawrence. *The Conserver Solution*. Toronto: Doubleday, 1978.

Visser, James. *The Farmer and a Third Option*. Edmonton, Alberta: Christian Farmers' Federation, 1976.

Ward, Barbara. *The Home of Man*. Toronto: McLennan & Stewart, 1976.